# DRAW SCIENCE

# Wild Animals

## By Nina Kidd

Lowell House House
Juvenile

Los Angeles

Contemporary Books
Chicago

*To Wade*

Reviewed and endorsed by Q. L. Pearce, author of *Giants of the Land, Giants of the Deep, Armadillos and Other Unusual Animals,* and the *Animal Footprints* series.

Requests for such permissions should be addressed to:
Lowell House Juvenile
2029 Century Park East, Suite 3290
Los Angeles, CA 90067

Publisher: Jack Artenstein
Executive Vice-President: Nick Clemente
Editor-in-Chief: Lisa Melton

Manufactured in the United States of America.

ISBN: 0-929923-90-1

10 9 8 7 6 5 4 3 2 1

# CONTENTS

# Drawing Tips

This book shows you how to draw 24 different wild animals. There are lots of different ways to draw, and here are just a few. You'll find some helpful hints throughout this book to help make your drawings the best they can be.

Before you begin, here are some tips that every aspiring artist should know!

- Use a large sheet of paper and make your drawing fill up the space. It's easier to see what you are doing, and you will have plenty of room to add details.

- When you are blocking in the large shapes, draw by moving your whole arm, not just your fingers.

- Experiment with different kinds of lines: do a light line, then gradually bear down for a wider, darker one. Try groups of lines, straight, crossing, curved, jagged. You'll find that just by changing the thickness of a line, your whole picture will look different!

- Remember every artist has his or her own style. Your picture shouldn't look exactly like the one in the book. It should reflect your own creativity.

- Most of all, have fun!

# What You'll Need

## PAPER

Many kinds of paper can be used, but some are better than others. For pencil drawing, avoid newsprint or rough papers because they don't erase well. Instead, use a large pad of bond paper (or a similar type of paper). The paper doesn't have to be thick, but it should be uncoated, smooth, and cold pressed. You can find bond paper at an art store. If you are using ink, a dull-finished, coated paper works best.

## PENCILS, CHARCOAL, AND PENS

A regular school pencil is fine for drawing, but try to use one with a soft lead. Pencils with a soft lead are labeled #2; #3 pencils have a hard lead. If you want a thicker lead, ask an art store clerk or an art teacher for an artist's drafting pencil.

4

Charcoal will give you a very black line, but it smudges easily and is hard to control in small drawings. If you want to use charcoal, start with a charcoal pencil of medium to hard grade. With it, you will be able to rub in shadows, then erase certain areas to make highlights.

If you want a smooth, thin ink line, try a rolling-point or a fiber-point pen. Art stores and larger stationery stores have them in a variety of line widths and fun, bright colors.

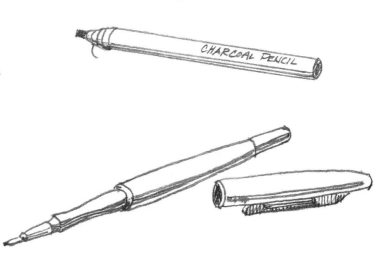

## ERASERS

An eraser is one of your most important tools! Besides removing unwanted lines and cleaning up smudges, erasers can be used to make highlights and textures. Get a soft plastic type (the white ones are good), or for very small areas, a gray kneaded eraser can be helpful. Try not to take off ink with an eraser because it will ruin the drawing paper. If you must take an ink line out of your picture, use liquid whiteout.

## OTHER HANDY TOOLS

Facial tissues are helpful for creating soft shadows—just go over your pencil marks with a tissue and rub it gently around the area you want smoothed out.

A square of metal window screen is another tool that can be used to make shadows. Hold it just above your paper and rub a soft pencil lead on it. Then rub the shavings from the pencil into the paper to make a smooth shadowed area in your picture. If you like, you can add a sharp edge to the shadow with your eraser.

You will also need a pencil sharpener, but if you don't have one, rub the side of your pencil point against a small piece of sandpaper to keep the point sharp.

# Backgrounds

Once you have completed a drawing, you may want to put your animal in a setting. An encyclopedia or some travel guides will show you what the plants and land look like where the animal lives. Or, use your imagination! Here are some suggestions for different settings.

## MAGAZINE BACKGROUNDS

If you like to cut and paste, ask your family for some old magazines you can cut up. If your animal lives in the jungle, cut out different trees and rocks. Or cut out different patterns, and cut them into the shapes of trees and rocks! This will give your picture an abstract, funky look. And you don't have to fill the entire page—just a few trees or some mountains in the background will give the impression of a whole scene.

## PAINTED BACKGROUNDS

You don't need a paintbrush to add *these* painted backgrounds! If you want to make an animal's footprints, dip the round end of a pencil eraser into some paint and print it on your drawing in groupings of four or five for footprints. For other shapes and textures, also try cut edges of corrugated board, the end of an old spool, or a cut piece of Styrofoam. Also try using crumpled wax paper or a paper towel. Be sure not to get them too wet or they won't work well.

## TEXTURED BACKGROUNDS

If you want to create a textured background, you'll need to draw your animal on a thin piece of paper. Grab a pencil with a thick lead and place a textured object (such as a thick-veined leaf) under the section of your paper where you want the texture to appear. Then rub evenly and lightly over the area with the side of your pencil lead. Try sandpaper, window screening, rough wood, pavement, a fine kitchen grater— anything you can imagine!

## SHADOWED BACKGROUNDS

By adding shadows in just the right places, your animals will leap off the page! Imagine where the shadow of your animal would fall underneath its tail, neck, and belly. Then fill in those places with dark pencil. If you need some help figuring out where a shadow might fall, experiment with your own shadow! Go outside and see where it falls during different times of the day. Notice, too, how long your shadow is. Depending on the time of day, a shadow may shrink or grow. If you wanted your animal to cast a morning shadow, the shadow would be very long. How would that shadow look at noon?

# Finishing Your Drawing

As you'll see with the wild animals in this book, different techniques result in very different looks. Artists use many finishing techniques to make their animals seem real. Here are some very useful techniques for giving your drawings a natural look.

## HATCHING

Hatching is a group of short, straight lines used to create a texture or a shadow. When you curve the hatching lines, you create a rounded look. This is handy when texturing an animal's legs, neck, or underside. When you draw the hatching lines close together, you create a dark shadow, such as with the underside and face of the deer. For very light shading, draw the lines shorter, thinner, and farther apart, as shown on the deer's back.

## CROSS-HATCHING

This technique gives your animal a wrinkled look. Start with an area of hatching, then crisscross it with a new set of lines. If you are drawing wrinkles on skin, make the lines a bit wobbly and uneven, just as creases in real skin would be. Take a look at the elephant to see how larger cross-hatching works well for big areas of skin, while smaller cross-hatching looks good in smaller areas, such as on the elephant's ears and feet.

## STIPPLE

When you want to give your drawing a different feel, try the stipple technique—and all you need are dots! This method works best with a pen, because unlike a pencil, a pen will make an even black dot by just touching the paper. You can make a shadow almost black just by placing the dots closer together. The stipple technique is very similar to the way photos are printed in newspapers and books. If you look through a magnifying glass at a picture in a newspaper, you will see very tiny dots.

Note that they are small and far apart in the light areas, and larger and closer to each other in the dark areas. Stipple is a good texture to use for the smooth-haired, spotted skin of a giraffe or for the fine-textured skin of a marine iguana.

## SMOOTH TONE

By using the side of your pencil, you can create a smooth texture on your creature. Start in the lighter areas with the side of the pencil, stroking very lightly and evenly. Put a little bit more pressure on your pencil as you move to the areas you want to be darker. If you want something even smoother, go back and rub the pencil with a facial tissue, but rub gently! If you get smudges in areas you want to stay white, simply remove them with an eraser. Try this smooth texture on the shark or (in combination with hatching) for the eagle as shown.

## SPECIALIZED FUR AND SKIN TEXTURES

Look at the crocodile and the polar bear to see even more ways to finish a drawing. The crocodile has squarish shapes to suggest scales. Notice how the squares get smaller on the legs and seem to curve around its legs and back. On its underside the lines are thicker to suggest a shadow.

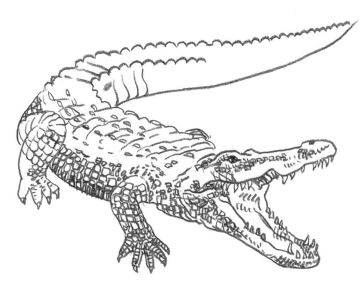

The polar bear has long, shaggy fur. Don't give its outline a hard edge; instead, indicate fur all around its body with fine strokes. Since the bear is white, keep the shadowed areas more delicate.

Now that you're armed with the basic drawing tools and techniques, you're ready to get started on the wild animals in this book. What's more, you'll learn as you draw! After each drawing step, you'll find some scientific information that is not only fun and interesting to know, but is also useful when it comes to drawing.

Throughout this book, too, you'll find special Drawing Tips that will aid your progress. Last, at the back of the book, are extra techniques and hints for using color, casting shadows, and placing animals in a scene—in short, making the most of your drawings.

# The Gorilla is the largest animal in the primate group, which includes monkeys, apes, and humans. Gorillas make an impressive

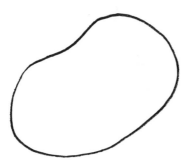

① Start by sketching a kidney-bean shape for the body. Your picture will eventually be an adult male gorilla.

*Gorillas usually live together in groups of 10 to 30 members. The groups are always led by a dominant male who protects the group.*

② Add the thick upper legs and upper arms. Also sketch in an egg shape for the face.

*There are three types of gorillas: the eastern and western lowland gorillas and the rare mountain gorilla. The gorilla's location and head shape determine which subspecies it belongs to.*

③ Next draw both the forearms and the lower legs, as well as the huge crest, or top, of the head.

*Gorillas have arms that are longer and stronger than their legs. The average gorilla's arms are more powerful than the strongest man's legs!*

**MORE SCIENCE:** Some zoos have been able to raise gorillas, and people in Africa are trying to set aside some forest land for them so these interesting and peaceful animals can survive.

**sight, especially the males, which can weigh from 300 to 500 pounds. Still, they are peaceful and intelligent creatures.**

④ Now draw the feet and the hands. Add the nose area and the diamond-shaped mouth, and sketch in a mask shape in the eye area.

*A similarity to humans can be found in the gorilla's hands and feet, which both have five digits. Gorillas do not walk upright, but on all fours. While the toes are kept flat, the fingers are curled under. This is called "knuckle walking."*

⑤ Pencil in the toes and toenails, eyes, nostrils, lips, and the ear. Erase the unnecessary lines around the face, legs, arms, shoulders, feet, and hands. Begin to suggest fur around the head, eyes, shoulder, elbow, and hand.

*Gorillas have much bigger jaws and teeth than humans do. They use their teeth to grind up the tough plant stalks they eat.*

⑥ Using short, dark strokes, add fur around the gorilla's body. The fur should be darker around the far leg, far arm, and the head. Color in the eyes. Detail the feet and hands with knuckle lines.

*All three types of gorillas live in rain forests and are endangered. Although laws have been passed to protect them from most poachers, their forest home is being cut down for farmland and lumber.*

# The Lion is one of the world's great cats. The male has a spectacular mane, a fitting crown for "the king of the jungle." The lion

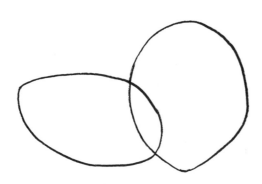

① Start your lion by drawing a long oval for the body and a large rounded shape for the mane.

*A male lion can weigh up to 500 pounds. Its powerful yet graceful body enables the cat to creep up on prey and surprise it.*

② Add three long shapes: two for the upper forelegs and one for the right hindleg.

*Lions often charge their prey and can cover a distance of 30 to 35 feet in a single leap.*

③ Next draw a curved, tapering tail, three small lower legs, and an upside-down egg shape for the face.

*The lion's face is longer than that of such smaller wild cats as the cheetah and puma, but its mouth is equipped with the same three kinds of teeth: large spiked canines in the front corners of its mouth to help the lion grab and hold onto its prey, small front teeth to snip off meat from bones, and large back teeth to chew the meat.*

**MORE SCIENCE:** The sometimes frightening roar of the male lion can be heard for miles. The female's roar is loud, too. It may sound frightening, but sometimes it is just a mother calling her cubs.

**lives on the grasslands of Africa and in the Gir Forest in India.**

④ Add the furry tip of the tail, four ovals for the paws, rounded ears, and a large W-shaped lower jaw.

*Like all cats, the lion keeps its claws hidden in a protective sheath in its paws, revealing them only to attack its prey or to sharpen them in preparation for a hunt.*

⑤ Now add toes, claws, eyes, teeth, a nose, and ear details. Connect and smooth the joints between the leg sections and erase all unnecessary lines. Draw jagged strokes around the mane and at the rear joints of the forelegs.

*Lions usually hunt at night. Their ears can hear sounds from up to a mile away. Their eyes, the largest of any meat-eating land animal, are designed to see exceptionally well in the dark.*

⑥ Finish your lion by shading the mane and adding fine texture lines for fur around its body and face. Fill in the eyes, nose, mouth, and ears. Shade the undersides of the body and limbs, especially the far rear leg.

*The lion's golden brown coat blends in with the dry grasses of the plains where it lives and hunts. This helps the great cat to sneak up on its prey without being seen.*

**DRAWING TIP:** You can learn a lot about this beautiful animal by studying a friend's or your own house cat. The lion's ears are shorter and rounded, and its legs and feet are heavier.

# The Giraffe is the tallest animal on Earth. The tallest one ever measured was 19 feet, 3 inches tall. This African animal's

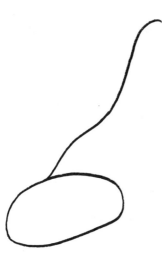

① First draw an oval-shaped body. Then sketch a curved line upward from the body to form the giraffe's long backbone.

*A giraffe's neck is made up of seven huge vertebrae bones. That's the same number as in a human's neck, but the giraffe's vertebrae may be 10 inches long!*

② Add a cone shape for the head, four long shapes for the upper legs, and a thin rectangle for the base of the tail. Notice that one of the back upper legs is higher than the body.

*Because the giraffe's legs are so long, each stride it takes is about 15 feet long. When it wants to take a drink from a stream or pond, it must spread its legs wide so its neck can bend down to reach the water.*

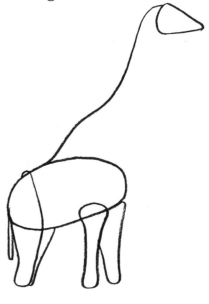

③ Now draw the tuft of the tail and the lower leg sections. Connect the base of the cone-shaped head with a line curving down to the body.

*When running, most animals push off with their hindlegs, but it relies more on its front legs. The giraffe's long legs enable it to run at speeds of up to 35 miles per hour.*

**MORE SCIENCE:** Because they can reach high into the trees where other plant eaters can't feed, giraffes can live side by side with animals such as zebras and antelopes, which eat food lower to the ground on the African plains.

**amazing neck accounts for nearly half that height.**

④ Sketch four small hooves and a leaf-shaped ear.

*Although the giraffe is a peaceful animal, if it has to, it will defend itself with its hard, sharp hooves by kicking. It can kill an attacker such as a lion with a single blow!*

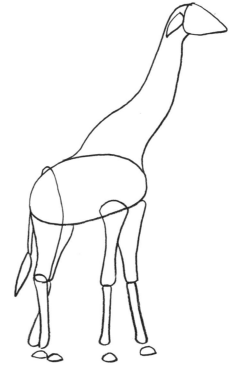

⑤ Draw two knobby-tipped horns at the top of the head. Add an eye and a nostril. Connect the hooves to the legs. Erase overlapping lines within the body, head, and limbs. Use two short lines to indicate splits in the hooves and shade in the tuft of the tail.

*A giraffe has a split hoof like a cow's, but its foot is over twice the length of a cow's foot.*

⑥ Shade in the eye, ear, and hooves. Add a short mane running down the back of its long neck. Now it's time to add the spots. They should be larger on the neck and body and smaller on the legs. Add detail to the face as shown.

*There are nine subspecies of giraffe. Each lives in its own geographical area in Africa, and each has a unique pattern of spots.*

# The Hippopotamus is a distant relative of the domestic pig. This hefty African mammal weighs

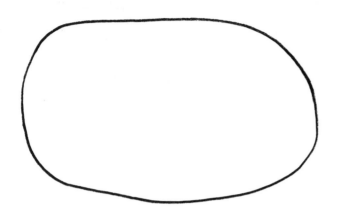

① To start your hippo, draw a wide bean-shaped body.

*The hippopotamus is the only large land mammal that is not endangered. Common hippos are 13 to 15 feet long.*

② Next draw a rounded square for the head. Add a small, stubby tail.

*The hippo's head takes up about one-third of its body length.*

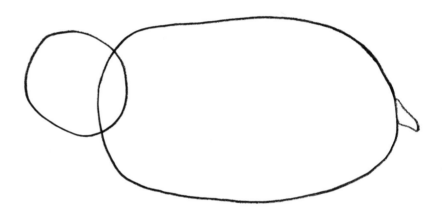

③ Overlap the visible thick and stubby legs with the body. Draw a teardrop-shaped muzzle and a squared-off, crescent-moon shape for the neck.

*The hippo's ears, eyes, and nostrils are all on top of its head. This makes it easy for the hippopotamus to see and breathe while almost totally submerged. This way, too, it can hide from its enemies.*

**MORE SCIENCE:** How long can you hold your breath? A hippo can remain completely underwater for 10 minutes or more at a time.

**between three and four tons. It loves the water and spends nearly all of its time in the lakes and rivers that are the hippo's home.**

④ Sketch in four feet, two circles for the eyes, and rectangular ears, including inner ear details.

*At night, hippos leave the safety and comfort of their watery homes to feed on grass.*

⑤ Connect and smooth the lines between the legs and feet. Then erase the unnecessary lines around the head area, the legs, and the neck. Add the eyes, toes and toenails, and nostril lines.

*Adult hippos have few natural enemies, but the males fight each other over leadership of the herd or space in the mud hole. Fighting hippos will use the two huge teeth in their lower jaw to gouge each other.*

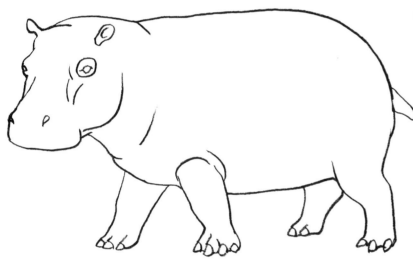

⑥ Finally, add texture to the hippopotamus's coarse, thick skin and use dark, short strokes around the head and limbs. With light, wispy strokes, create bristles on the tail, whiskers on the snout, and light coloring around the body.

*A hippo's hide can be a full two inches thick. That thickness protects the animal when it's being attacked. Blows that would be deadly to a thinner-skinned creature are no problem for the hippo.*

# The Rhinoceros is a distant cousin of the horse. The rhino evolved 50 million years ago. All but one of the five

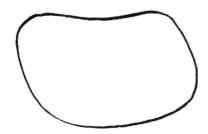

① Begin drawing a rounded, rectangular body.

*The rhino, though heavy, can reach a running speed of 30 miles per hour for short distances.*

② Now draw an irregular shape connected to the body for the neck.

*A rhino's foot has an odd number of toes—three. The horse has an odd number, too, but only one. Its single toe—the hoof—evolved from a large middle toe that's very similar to the rhino's middle toe!*

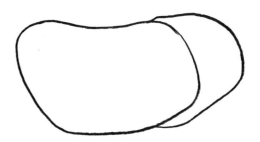

③ Overlap a bean-shaped head with the neck. Add the four upper legs.

*Although the rhino can be fierce in protecting its young or its place in the watering hole, it is normally a placid and shy animal.*

**MORE SCIENCE:** Black rhinos live in southern and eastern Africa. Rhinos must visit a water source at least once a day, and they often spend the hottest part of the day wallowing in mud to stay cool. The layer of mud also protects them from biting insects.

species of rhinos are nearly extinct. Rhinos live in Africa, India, Java, and Sumatra. The rhinoceros shown here is the black rhino of Africa.

④ Next connect the tail to the larger hindleg. Add lower legs and feet. Draw the ears and a long, triangular horn. Sketch in a smaller horn behind it.

*A rhino's horns are different from a cow's horns. A rhino's horn is made of a bundle of hollow fibers similar to hairs, held together with keratin, the same material as in your fingernails.*

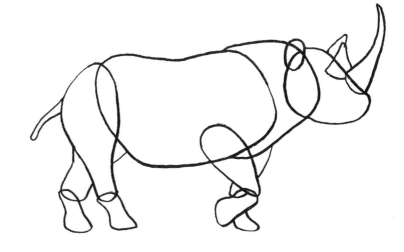

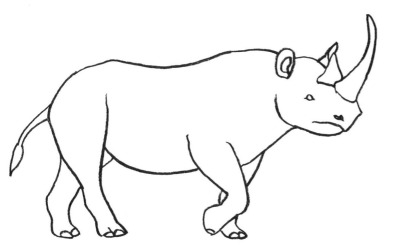

⑤ Sketch small semicircles for the toenails and eye. Add a small nostril and a mouth line. Then add detail to the inner ear. Indicate a tuft of hair on the end of the tail and erase all unnecessary lines throughout.

*The black rhinoceros grows to about 10 to 12 feet long and about six feet high at the shoulder. It weighs from two thousand to three thousand pounds, and its front horn can grow to an amazing four feet long.*

⑥ Fill in the ear, eye, and nose of your rhinoceros. Indicate hair around its ears and on the end of its tail. Shade in the rhino's underside and around the face and horns. Draw in texture around the body and legs. Last, add a long piece of twig that the rhino is munching on.

*This species of African rhino may be called "black," but it is actually dark gray. It has a pointed upper lip, which it curls around leaves and twigs to pull from plants.*

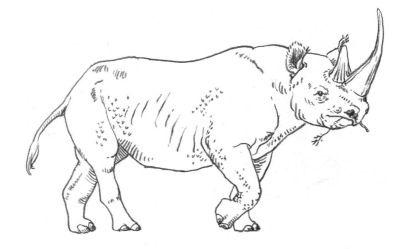

**DRAWING TIP:** Unlike the elephant, the rhino has a thick, bumpy skin that forms deep creases at its hips, shoulders, and neck. You can show the skin's thickness by drawing curved ridges where the skin creases.

# The Elephant is the largest living land animal. There are two species of elephant. One lives in Africa, and one lives in India.

① Begin by drawing a semicircle for the elephant's body.

*The elephant has a trunk that is both a very long nose and part of its upper lip. There are two nasal passages in the trunk. An elephant uses its trunk to breathe, touch, smell, eat, shower, and move or pick up objects.*

② Next draw the head and trunk, the tail, and the upper parts of the legs.

*The elephant also uses its trunk by drawing in a snoutful of water, then spraying it into its mouth. The trunk can hold about two gallons of water at a time.*

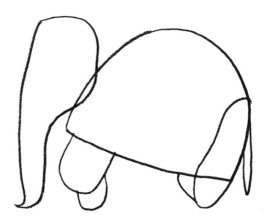

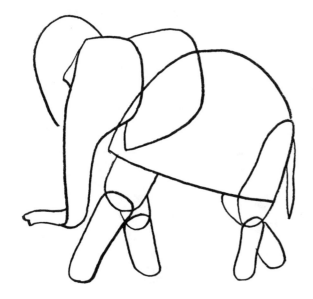

③ Create ears with semicircles on either side of the elephant's head. In the animal's right ear draw an eyebrow ridge. Add the trunk tip and the lower parts of the legs.

*The African elephant uses its big ears to help it stay cool in the hot temperatures. When it flaps its ears, the blood vessels within are cooled by the breeze.*

**MORE SCIENCE:** An elephant mother carries its calf for 22 months before it is born. An elephant baby can weigh up to 200 pounds at birth, and it can walk just a few minutes after being born! It nurses from its mother for more than two years.

**Both species are endangered, mostly because their habitat is shrinking and because poachers kill them for their ivory tusks.**

④ Add tusks on either side of its trunk and a tassel to the tail. Use small semicircles for the feet.

*An African bull elephant can weigh more than six tons, or as much as 80 average-sized men put together.*

⑤ Sketch in eyes, toenails, and sheath lines over the upper end of each tusk. Erase all unneeded lines to create a smooth outline.

*Male and female African elephants have tusks, but the male's tusks are longer and thicker and can grow to more than 10 feet long.*

⑥ Shade in the eyes, ears, and toenails. Use hatch lines to define wrinkles in the face, body, and legs. Add smaller lines on the trunk, around the ears, and on the body.

*To warn off another animal, an elephant will make a trumpeting sound and shake its head. When an elephant attacks, it curls its trunk, spreads its ears wide, and charges.*

**DRAWING TIP:** The legs and feet of this animal are built for carrying a great weight. Emphasize the elephant's huge size by using thick, heavy outlines and dark shadows.

# The Zebra of Africa is closely related to the horse, wild ass, and donkey.

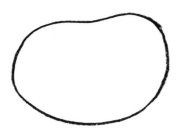

① Begin by drawing a jelly bean shape, which will be the zebra's body.

*Not all zebras are black and white. Zebras may have brown, gray, or tan stripes.*

② Then draw a thick neck. Sketch in the four upper legs.

*Each species of zebra has its own typical stripe pattern, and within a given species each zebra's pattern varies enough to make the animal unique. All zebras' stripes protect them from predators, such as lions. In the low light of evening, the stripe pattern on a zebra breaks up its visual outline, making it difficult for a lion to spot.*

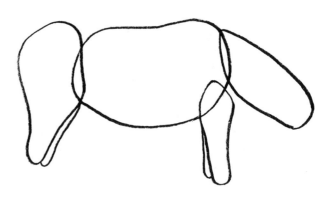

③ Draw thin rectangular shapes for the lower sections of the legs. Add a circle to the base of the neck for the forehead and jaw. Don't forget to add a tail.

*The zebra stands from four to five feet high at the shoulder and weighs from 500 to 600 pounds.*

**MORE SCIENCE:** Zebras are placid and harmless as they graze. But when provoked, they can be dangerous. Although on the whole, zebras are not considered to be endangered, several subspecies are threatened because of poaching and shrinking habitats.

**It is shorter than most horses and has a brushy, upright mane.**

④ Draw a curved line from the forehead to the body. This will be the outline of the zebra's mane. Add a stubby cone shape for a muzzle and small wedges for hooves.

*A zebra's body is made for running. It has a strong heart and lungs and powerful hindquarters. A zebra can run 50 miles per hour for short distances and 35 miles per hour for long distances.*

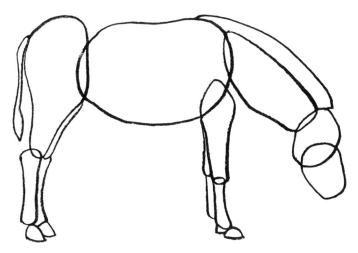

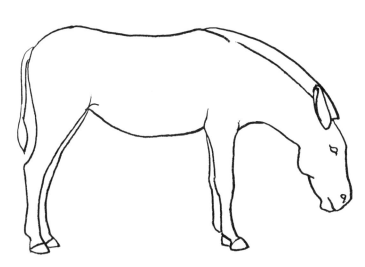

⑤ On the head add the eye, nostril, mouth, and jaw. Draw ears next to the mane outline. Erase all unnecessary lines, then smooth out the lines between the joints.

*A zebra's ears are long like a donkey's. When a zebra is relaxed and alert, it holds its ears straight up. When afraid, it strains its ears forward, and it flattens them back against its head in anger.*

⑥ Shade in curved stripes that appear to wrap around the body, legs, and face. Fill in the eyes and nostril. Add detail to the tail and hooves, and indicate a bristly mane with short, dark strokes. Finally, add a small patch of grass for your wild zebra to graze on.

*Some zebras whinny softly like a horse, while other species grunt hoarsely and whistle.*

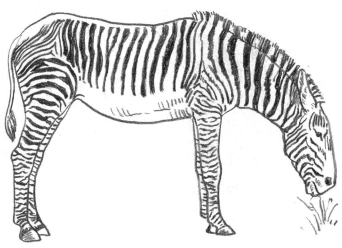

**DRAWING TIP:** Each zebra has its own stripe pattern. However, the stripe pattern on most zebras is strongest along the backbone and fronts of the legs, then fades and blurs slightly as it turns to the belly and inner sides of the legs.

# The Nile Crocodile is one member in a group of the world's largest reptiles. Some crocodiles measure

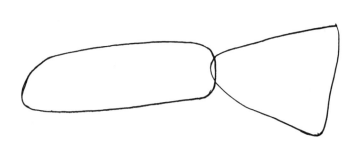

① To begin, draw a long, almond-shaped body and a triangular shape for the head with its huge, open mouth.

*A fully grown Nile crocodile can weigh 800 pounds or more. As its name suggests, this crocodile lives in the warm-water rivers and lakes of northern Africa, especially in the Nile River.*

② Extend two curved lines from the head through the body and connect them above the rest of the animal. This will create the crocodile's ridged back and huge tail. Draw two shapes for the thick upper legs as shown.

*A crocodile's tail is longer than the rest of its body. The crocodile pushes itself along with its tail underwater, and it may also use its tail to stun its prey by quickly snapping it.*

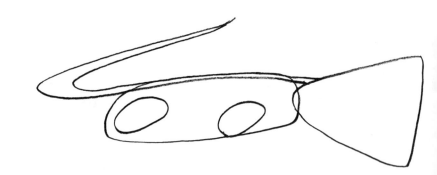

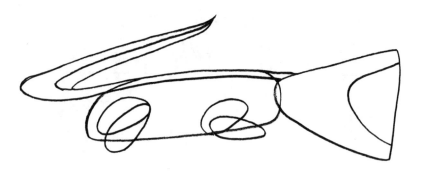

③ Then draw the underside of the tail, add a semicircle for the gaping mouth, and sketch in two shapes for the lower legs on the crocodile's right side.

*Crocodiles eat fish. However, when a land animal comes to drink at a riverbank, the crocodile may leap out of the water and grab it.*

**MORE SCIENCE:** Crocodiles, alligators, and other crocodilians are endangered for two reasons: loss of habitat and hunters who kill them for their skins, which are made into boots, shoes, pocketbooks, and belts.

④  Sketch wavy lines within the snout to define the jaw. Add eye bumps and a throat line connecting the jaw to the body.

*Even when a crocodile's mouth is closed, almost all its teeth are still showing on the outside.*

⑤  Begin to detail the eye, nostril, bumpy nose tip, sharp teeth, toes, and claws. Erase all joint lines to smooth the outline throughout the body, legs, and tail.

*Lying quietly in the water, the crocodile looks like a water-soaked log. A submerged crocodile can still see and breathe because its eyes and nostrils are high on the top of its head. This makes it easy for the crocodile to sneak up unnoticed on its prey.*

⑥  Draw in ridged scales and hatch lines for skin texture from the toes to the tail. Add lighter shading to the head and fill in the eye.

*A crocodile's skin is made up of tough protective plates that are held together by more flexible skin.*

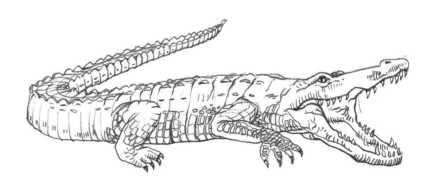

**DRAWING TIP:** As you draw the crocodile's stiff, rectangular plates, remember that the plates on top of the animal face upward. You need to draw them narrower than the plates on the side of the animal because you're seeing these upward-facing plates in profile.

# The Ostrich is the tallest bird in the world. It may not surprise you that the nine-foot-tall, 300-pound ostrich can't fly, but it

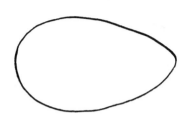

① Start your ostrich by drawing an egg-shaped body.

*Scientists think that the ostrich is a descendant of another flightless bird that lived in prehistoric times and was itself a descendant of a dinosaur.*

② Sketch in a long, thin neck, a fan-shaped tail, and two drumstick shapes for this bird's powerful upper legs.

*The ostrich uses its long neck to peer high above the tall grass, keeping watch for lions and other predators while it hunts for rodents and insects to eat.*

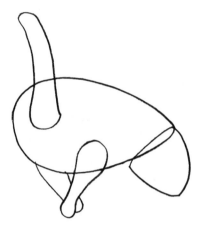

③ Next draw a small pear-shaped head on top of the neck. Cross two thin oblongs to make the lower legs.

*The ostrich was once hunted for its feathers. People wanted the soft plumes to decorate their clothing and hats.*

**MORE SCIENCE:** Ostriches were first tamed thousands of years ago. Today people may raise them on farms for their plumes or even ride them in races.

**can run 40 miles per hour—faster than any other two-legged animal. It can also knock out a human with its powerful kick.**

④ Add a line through the upper part of the head to indicate the beak. Sketch in the eyes and add large feet.

*The ostrich is the only bird with just two toes. Its feet have heavy pads on the bottom to protect them as the ostrich runs.*

⑤ Now sketch in lines for the nostril, beak, toes, and claws. Indicate tail feathers with an uneven outline as shown. Connect the back of the head to the base of the neck and erase all unnecessary joint lines.

*An ostrich uses its wings to turn quickly when running. Spurlike claws that are hidden on its wingtips can be used to fight off its enemies.*

⑥ Use dark, wavy strokes to create textured tail and body feathers. Notice how the strokes become thicker near the tail. Lightly shade in the head and neck with short diagonal lines for downy feathers. Draw in horizontal ridges on the feet for a scaly texture. Fill in the eyes and shade in the claws.

*The ostrich's large eyes give it excellent long-distance vision over the African grasslands. A thick fringe of lashes protects its eyes from the dust.*

**DRAWING TIP:** Look at a chicken's foot to help you see how the ostrich's claws grow. You can also look at the texture of the chicken's foot to find out what scaly ostrich skin looks like.

# The Giant Panda was unknown in the Western world until about 130 years ago. For many years, scientists

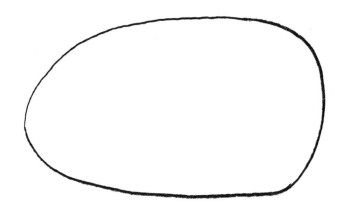

① First draw an oblong shape for the panda's large body.

*One hint that giant pandas are closely related to bears is their appearance: their round bodies and heads make them look very similar to bears.*

② Next sketch the circular head and three thick leg shapes. The fourth leg should be suggested by adding a thin triangle.

*Giant pandas have powerful jaw muscles and broad teeth, both of which are typical of meat eaters. While it does sometimes hunt small mammals, birds, and fish, the panda's main source of food is the bamboo. A panda may eat more than 80 pounds of bamboo per day!*

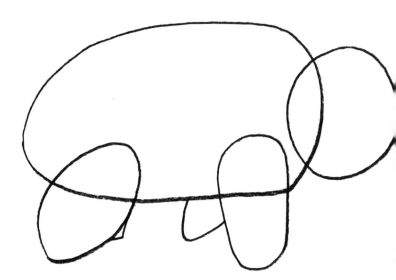

③ Add feet, a triangular neck, a muzzle, rounded ears, and two eye patches.

*The giant panda's paws are like those of a bear, except that it has a special fleshy pad under each forepaw, which the panda uses like a thumb. This enables the mammal to grasp the slim bamboo stalks and shoots it eats. It uses its mouth to tear leaves off the stalks.*

**MORE SCIENCE:** The giant panda's rear legs aren't as powerful as its front legs. Perhaps this makes running a difficult matter for the animal. Even when it is being chased, the giant panda seldom breaks beyond a shambling trot.

**were unsure whether the giant panda was more closely related to raccoons or to bears. Now, after close study, the giant panda is considered to be a kind of bear.**

④ Smooth out the lines between the head and body and around the face and legs. Add the eyes, nose, mouth, and the toes and claws. Erase any unnecessary lines and begin to sketch in fur around the head and ear.

*Despite their bulky appearance, giant pandas are very limber. They will often sit erect on their haunches, raise up one hindpaw, and rest one of their cheeks on the paw!*

⑤ Now add in the black fur that makes the panda unique. Using short, dark strokes, shade in the legs, the shoulder area, and the eye patches. Darken the ear and the nose, and add fur lines around the body and face.

*The black and white fur of a giant panda is very stiff and coarse. The thick fur keeps the panda warm and protects it from the prickly foliage of its jungle home.*

# The Tiger

once ranged from Turkey in the west, southern Asia in the south, and Japan in the northeast. It is one of the largest of

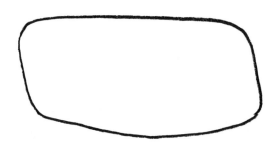

① First draw a rounded, rectangular body.

*Though weight varies widely from tiger to tiger, a male may grow up to 10 feet long and may weigh 650 pounds or more.*

② Slightly overlap the circular head shape with a corner of the body. Draw two large shapes for the tiger's upper hindlegs.

*Most tiger species live in damp, humid places. They like to cool down by taking a swim and seem to enjoy water more than any other great cat. The largest of the tigers, the Siberian, lives the farthest north and must contend with snowy winters. Its coat is paler and shaggier than that of other tigers.*

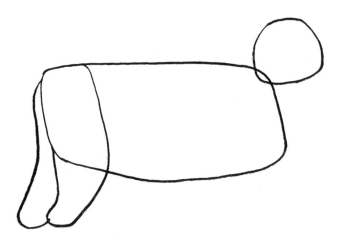

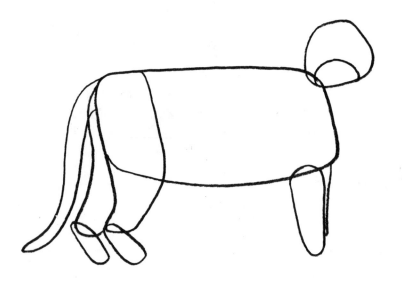

③ Add a long, tapering tail. Draw in the upper forelegs and lower hindlegs. Now add a half circle to the head for the muzzle.

*Although the tiger can leap up to 18 feet, it doesn't actually leap onto its prey. Instead, it attacks from the side or back and uses its forelimbs to knock the prey off balance. With large prey, the tiger may reach up and grip the back of the animal's neck with its teeth and claws, bearing down with the weight of its body to take the prey down.*

**MORE SCIENCE:** To survive, an adult tiger eats about 70 deer or similar animals every year. Males have large territories of up to 40 square miles that overlap the territories of several females. The territories of tigers of the same sex never overlap.

**the wild cats. The tiger is the national symbol of India and one of the best known animals in the world.**

④ Next position the paws at the base of each foreleg. Connect the head to the body with two wavy lines for the neck as shown. Add triangular ears.

*Adult tigers generally live and hunt alone, although cubs stay with their mothers for about one year or even longer. Mother tigers teach their cubs to kill prey by demonstration. A mother tiger will bring down a small animal near the cub and let the cub assist her in the kill.*

⑤ Now draw in the details of the face: the eyes, the nose, the lower jaw (with teeth), and the whisker area. Add toe lines to the paws. Pencil in fur fringe on the body's underside and lower legs. Erase unnecessary lines within the head, body, and legs.

*All species of the tiger are now extremely endangered.*

⑥ Create an interesting stripe pattern for your tiger. Notice how the stripes get thinner near the front of the tiger. Fill in its eyes and mouth, and add whiskers. Sketch in more fur along the underside and around the face, ears, and shoulder.

*A tiger's stripe pattern may range from pale tan stripes on a white background to black stripes on a tawny brown background. Each tiger's stripe pattern is different—it may even vary from one <u>side</u> of a tiger to the other!*

31

# The Polar Bear is one of the largest land predators on Earth. This dominant Arctic animal can grow up to 11 feet in

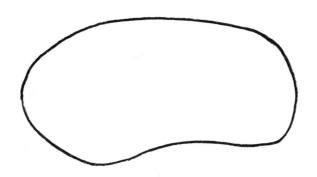

① To begin your polar bear, draw a long kidney bean shape for the body.

*Under a polar bear's skin is a thick layer of fat called blubber. The blubber keeps the bear warm, even during long swims in the Arctic Ocean's icy waters.*

② Add an oval shape for the head and neck, another for the upper foreleg, and two large, rounded shapes for the upper hindlegs.

*The polar bear's elongated snout gives it a better sense of smell. Its sense of smell is so extraordinary that the bear can sniff out a seal 20 miles away, or even one in its den three feet beneath the snowpack.*

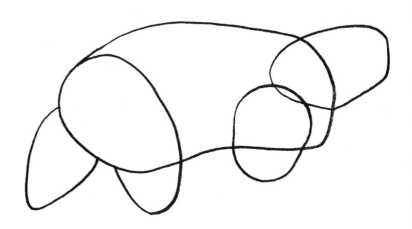

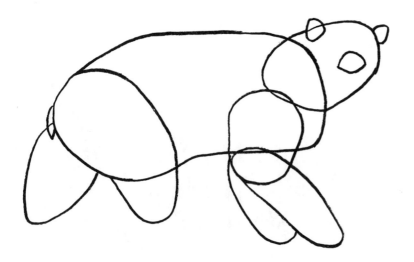

③ Next sketch in the lower forelegs and a small tail. Add a rounded shape for the muzzle and two small triangles for the ears.

*An excellent fisherman, the polar bear can stick its head in shallow water and scan the seafloor for fish or crabs. It can dive to depths of up to 15 feet and stay submerged for up to two minutes.*

**MORE SCIENCE:** During the winter a female polar bear usually gives birth to one or two cubs. In late spring, the cubs leave the den to accompany their mother on short hunting trips. They will not hunt on their own until the following year.

**length and weigh up to 1,300 pounds. Standing on its hindlegs, a full grown male may be taller than the average living room!**

④ Draw two short forepaws, two longer hindpaws, and two small eyes. Add a nose to the muzzle, as well as a curved line for the mouth.

*A polar bear sometimes uses its powerful paws to swipe fish out of the water and more often to attack large prey, such as seals and walruses. One paw can be a full 12 inches across.*

⑤ Connect the right hindleg to its paw and smooth the joints between the legs and feet. Erase all overlapping lines in the legs, body, and head. Sketch in the inner ears and add small strokes on the paws for toes and claws.

*In the fall, a pregnant female polar bear tunnels out a den in a snowbank. There she retires for the winter, safe and warm, to give birth to her cubs.*

⑥ Use short, dark strokes to create thick, shaggy fur around this mammal's body and use longer strokes around its legs. Shade in the areas around the eyes and muzzle, as well as around the ears and nose.

*A polar bear's thick coat provides warmth and protection from the ice world in which it lives.*

# The Raccoon is a medium-sized mammal that is found only in North and Central America. Its name comes from the

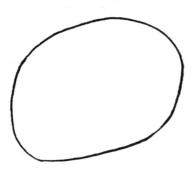

① Begin by drawing a rounded shape for the raccoon's body.

*Raccoons may weigh anywhere from 10 pounds to more than 30 pounds. They grow up to three feet in length, not including their 16-inch-long tails.*

② Next draw a fan-shaped head that overlaps the body. To create the back haunch and upper legs, add three shapes as shown.

*Raccoons have an excellent sense of touch. They like to feel along the muddy bottom of streams to locate food. Some of their favorite foods are crayfish, fish, worms, frogs, and turtles. They also eat nuts, corn, and other grains.*

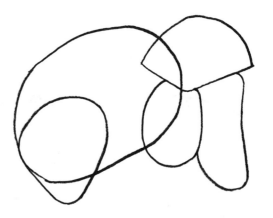

③ Now draw a long sausage-shaped tail. Overlap the shapes of the lower forelegs with the upper legs. Add rounded triangles for ears.

*A raccoon's thick and furry tail has between five and seven light gray bands.*

**MORE SCIENCE:** Trappers and early settlers in North America once used raccoon furs as money. Raccoon hats were worn by explorers such as Davy Crockett. Today, raccoons are still hunted for their furs, which are made into coats, pocketbooks, collars, and hats. Luckily, there are so many raccoons that they are not in danger of extinction, despite the great demand for their furs.

**Algonquin Indian word *arakhun*, meaning "he scratches with his hands." The raccoon is a very distant relative of the bear.**

④ Sketch two thin, oblong shapes for the hindfeet and two small circles for the forepaws. Use slightly wavy lines to form the eye patches, which are sometimes called the face mask, and add a small nose.

*A raccoon's forepaws have five "fingers." With its forepaws a raccoon can hold food easily. Even without an opposable thumb it can pick up small and delicate objects.*

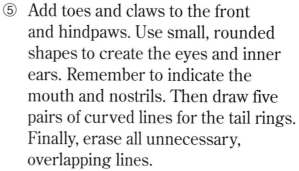

⑤ Add toes and claws to the front and hindpaws. Use small, rounded shapes to create the eyes and inner ears. Remember to indicate the mouth and nostrils. Then draw five pairs of curved lines for the tail rings. Finally, erase all unnecessary, overlapping lines.

*A raccoon's thick fur hides a strong body. When cornered, a raccoon is a match for even a fairly large dog. But raccoons don't usually like to fight, and they will often scramble up a tree to avoid it.*

⑥ Color in your raccoon's eyes and nose, and add whiskers. Sketch light, thin strokes for fur texture and fill in the tail rings, inner ears, and the eye mask with darker, bolder strokes. Add a fish in the raccoon's paws—one of its favorite meals!

*Raccoons vary in color from light tan to dark gray, and their fur is light-tipped. Raccoons live throughout the United States (except Hawaii and Alaska), but you may not have seen them because they are mainly active at night.*

35

# The Moose is the largest member of the deer family. Perhaps what most distinguishes this North American mammal is its pair

① First draw a round body to begin your moose.

*The adult male moose, called a bull, may be as tall as seven feet at the shoulder, which is taller than most professional basketball players.*

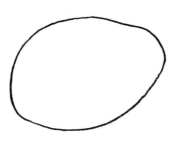

② Next draw a thick neck connected to the body and four upper legs.

*The moose's long legs help it run at a surprising 35 miles per hour.*

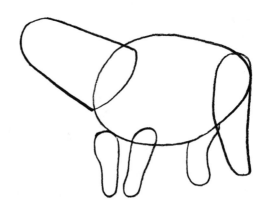

③ Sketch three long, rounded shapes for the muzzle and two antler outlines. Notice how the shape for the moose's right antler is not connected to the rest of the animal. Add the thin lower legs.

*The moose has a bulbous, down-turned muzzle. Its long upper lip helps the animal pull up the water plants it likes to eat.*

**MORE SCIENCE:** Moose can be very short tempered. You can sometimes tell when a moose is about to charge: it raises the thick mane of hair on its neck.

**of majestic antlers. The name moose comes from the Algonquin Indian word *musee*, which means "twig eater." Moose eat only plants.**

④ Now draw small, wedge-shaped hooves and two ears on top of its head. Add curved lines for the chin, eyebrow, and shoulder hump. Sketch the triangular dewlap, which is a flap of skin that hangs down from the moose's jaw and neck area.

*Moose live in the northern continental United States, Canada, and Alaska.*

⑤ Sketch in the hoof splits, the nostril, and the antler prongs. Smooth out the moose's shape and connect the antler and hooves to the rest of the animal. Erase any unnecessary lines.

*The bull moose's antlers are the largest of any animal in the deer family. Its antlers may grow to be six feet across and weigh up to 90 pounds.*

⑥ Use short, thick strokes for coarse fur around the ears, eyes, and dewlap. Draw in longer fur on the shoulders, the neck, and the underside of the moose's body. Add thinner shading strokes on the face and legs. Fill in the eye and nostril, and your moose is complete.

*The moose's fur is thick enough to withstand the harsh cold of winter. As spring approaches, the coat thins out, then thickens again with the coming of the cool autumn.*

# The Bighorn Sheep lives wild in the high, rugged country from Canada in the north to the western United States in the south. The American

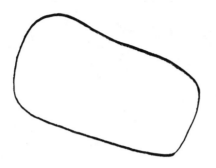

① Begin by drawing a rectangular body with the corners rounded.

*The bighorn sheep has a wide chest, broad hindquarters, and sturdy legs that allow it to jump and run among steep cliffs at high elevations.*

② Next draw a triangular head and connect it to the body with a short line. Add the four upper legs.

*The wild sheep has several enemies: the wolf, puma, and coyote, as well as the human hunter who wants the curved horns of the sheep as a wall trophy.*

③ Now sketch slim lower legs, a connecting lower neckline, and a circular outline for the ram's left horn.

*The sheep's horns grow from a base of tapered bone on the animal's head. Bighorn sheep do not shed their horns as deer shed their antlers. Instead, the horns continue to grow throughout their lives.*

**MORE SCIENCE:** The mature American bighorn can weigh up to 300 pounds. Both male and female sheep have horns: the female's horns are shorter and uncurved. She uses them to protect her lambs.

**bighorn is one of five related groups of wild sheep worldwide. The Spanish explorer, Coronado, first sighted this American wild sheep in the 1500s.**

④ Draw triangles for the hooves. Add the ram's right horn on the side of its head.

*At mating time, rival males will fight over females, butting their heads and locking horns, but the sheep generally use their horns defensively.*

⑤ Pencil in the eyes, nose, mouth, and the left horn. Erase all unneeded lines on the hooves, body, legs, head, and horns.

*Like the growth rings of a tree, a ram's horn rings indicate periods of abundance and scarcity of food for the ram. The skull and horns of a mature male American bighorn can weigh up to 40 pounds!*

⑥ Draw bold, short ridge lines on the horns and body. Shade in the eyes and the nose. Finally, add a ground line for the sheep to stand on.

*Bighorn sheep range in color from dark brown to pale tan, but all have white on their chins, undersides, and backs of their legs. Their horns are a muddy gold color.*

# The Bison is a wild relative of the domestic cow and is the largest of the land animals found in North America. At one time millions of bison roamed the great plains of the United States and

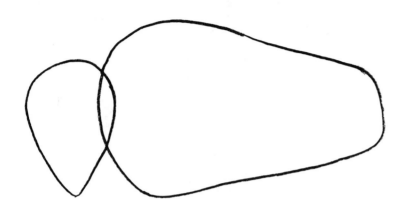

① First draw a long, pear-shaped body. Overlap the larger end of the body with a teardrop-shaped head.

*The bull bison (shown here) can reach six feet tall at the shoulder.*

② Next draw the small muzzle, the upper legs, and a long, thin tail.

*One distinctive feature of the bison is its high-humped shoulders, which connect its strong neck muscles to the animal's powerful forelegs. When a bison charges, it uses its head as a battering ram and is capable of knocking over dead trees as thick as six inches.*

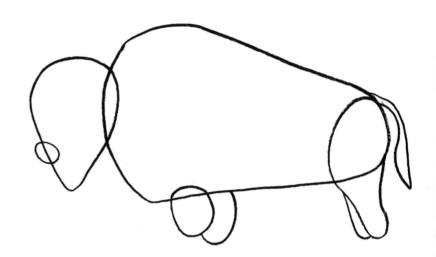

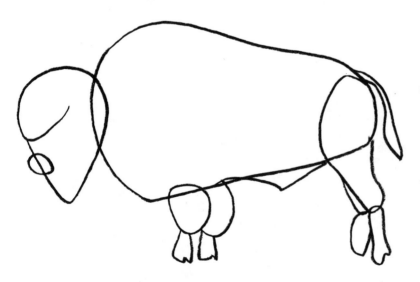

③ Add a large forehead line, four lower legs, and an outline for the bison's underside.

*Though it looks slow and clumsy, the bison can gallop at 35 miles per hour or more.*

**MORE SCIENCE:** Bison are fierce and unpredictable. When they bellow, it is time to retreat and get out of their way!

**Canada.** Although by the mid-1900s their numbers were seriously reduced, today populations of bison are growing again because of conservation efforts.

④ Draw wedge-shaped hooves. Indicate the ear, horn, chin, and beard.

*Both male and female bisons have permanent horns that have a bony core. The horns continue to grow all their lives.*

⑤ Add an eye, a nostril, and hoof tips. With ruffle lines, indicate hair around the tail, the two front legs, the shoulders, the chest, and the bison's head. Erase all unnecessary and overlapping lines between body parts.

*Like domestic cattle, the bison is a grazing animal. It spends most of its day resting and thoroughly chewing its food. Bison also live in herds.*

⑥ With thick, slanting strokes, indicate the coarse, wooly hair on the bison's head, chest, and forequarters. Use lighter strokes to shade in the rest of the body. Fill in the eye and add texture to the horn and hooves. To complete your bison, sketch in light fur behind its hooves and on its underside.

*There are two subspecies of American bison: the plains and the wood bison. The head, shoulders, and forelegs of both these species are covered with dark brown hair that is 10 inches long.*

**DRAWING TIP:** Study a picture of beef cattle to help you understand how the head, legs, and feet of this animal look. Don't hesitate to make the shoulders tall and the muscles on the bison's legs stand out.

# The White-Tailed Deer is just one of the several dozen species of deer found throughout the world. Abundant and

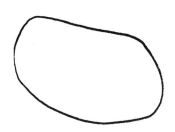

① First draw a jelly bean shape for the body.

*This deer's body is angular with slender legs, which help it to run and leap quickly through brush.*

② Next draw a rounded square for the head. Connect it to the body with a right-angle stroke for the neck. Add the upper sections of the legs.

*A deer's fur, which may change with the seasons, can be many different colors: red, brown, tan, gray, or black. Changing fur color helps the deer to hide in the forests from hunters and wild animals who prey upon them.*

③ Sketch long, thin rectangles for the lower parts of the legs. Add a muzzle.

*Deer are remarkable jumpers. Some have been known to leap over walls or fences eight feet high.*

**MORE SCIENCE:** Deer antlers are the fastest growing parts of any animal. A deer grows new antlers to replace its old ones every year.

**widespread, deer live in all kinds of climates, ranging from the cold of the Arctic to the heat of the tropical jungles. The white-tailed deer lives in North, Central, and South America.**

④ Draw a line from the muzzle to the body with a long, curved stroke. Add triangular ears and four small hooves. Indicate a tail on the deer.

*A deer depends upon its oversized ears to hear and detect the first signs of danger.*

⑤ Pencil in the eyes, nose, mouth, and small antlers. Indicate the splits in the hooves. Erase all unnecessary lines to create a smooth outline. Begin to add details to the ears and tail.

*It is most likely that deer communicate with each other by scent. The scent glands in their legs leave traces on shrubs. But some researchers have noted that deer feeding in groups will softly grunt and bleat to each other.*

⑥ Shade in the eyes, nose, hooves, and antlers as shown. Use short, dark strokes to give texture to the deer's coat on its legs, body, head, and tail.

*Of the white-tailed deer, only the males have antlers.*

**DRAWING TIP:** Imagine how the deer's coat would look up close. Your short texture strokes should look as if they lie on the curved surfaces of the animal's sides and legs.

# The Skunk lives both in North and South America. While each of the dozen or so species of skunks has a different black-and-

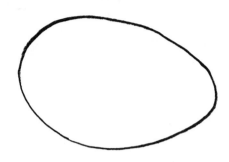

① First draw an egg-shaped body.

*This North American striped skunk has short legs and a wide body. It lives on the ground.*

② Next draw a petal-shaped tail on top of the body and a triangular head on the bottom.

*Under its fur, a skunk's skin has the same black-and-white pattern as seen on the fur.*

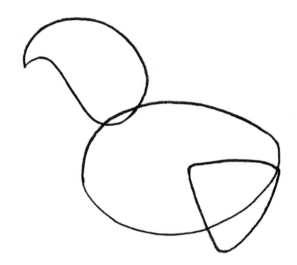

③ Now add the tip of the tail and three short legs.

*The scientific name for skunk is* mephitis, *which means "bad odor"! Using the strong muscles located under its tail, a skunk will squirt a smelly musk to ward off an attacker.*

**MORE SCIENCE:** The skunk's musk (the base of its strong-smelling defensive spray) was once used as a basic ingredient for perfumes. Today many perfumes are made with an artificial substitute.

**white pattern, all skunks have black heads with white stripes between the eyes.**

④ Add small, rounded shapes for the eyes, ears, nose, and two forefeet.

*Skunks aren't the only living things to use a bad smell to defend itself. Some other mammals as well as certain beetles discourage predators with their strong smells.*

⑤ Sketch in the claws and the inner ears. Add a thick body stripe and a smaller stripe down the middle of the skunk's head. You can give your skunk any kind of pattern you'd like, but remember that all skunks have a white forehead stripe. Don't forget to add fur lines around the paws. Erase all unnecessary lines.

*Farmers are glad to have skunks around because they eat pests such as grasshoppers, beetles, snails, and field mice.*

⑥ With dark, heavy strokes, shade in fur to create a black-and-white pattern. Fill in the eyes, nose, inner ears, and claw tips. To finish your skunk, add light, textured fur strokes around its whole body.

*The skunk sleeps during much of the cold winter, living off its thick layer of fat. In February or March it leaves its den to mate. By May or June, the mother skunk gives birth and usually has about five babies called kittens.*

**DRAWING TIP:** When you draw a skunk's long fur, try using quick, curved pencil strokes, making each stroke thicker at the base.

# The Harpy Eagle lives in the rain forests of South America. One of the largest of all eagles, it is one of

① Begin by drawing a leaf shape for the body.

*The female Harpy eagle is larger than the male. Female Harpy eagles are three feet long from head to tail, and they weigh between 16 and 20 pounds.*

② Next add a rounded square for the head, a smaller leaf shape inside the body for the wing, and a J shape below the wing, which will become the upper leg.

*Like all flying birds, Harpy eagles have hollow bones. This helps keep their bodies light.*

③ Now draw the thin lower legs, the tail, and the triangular beak.

*The Harpy eagle uses its powerful beak to rip apart the flesh of its prey. Its most common prey are monkeys, tree porcupines, and sloths.*

**MORE SCIENCE:** The Harpy eagle's short, broad wings help it maneuver through the forest at speeds between 35 and 50 miles per hour.

**the world's strongest birds of prey.**

④ Sketch two rounded shapes for the bird's feet. Then add the farthest wingtip and the crest feathers that stick out from the top of its head. Detail the hooked beak.

*The Harpy is one of the crested eagles. When it is angry or excited, the feathers on the back of its head stand up.*

⑤ Draw a few feathers around the head, thick toes, curved claws, the eyes, and the eyeridge lines over them. Add a dot for the nostril. Erase unnecessary lines around the body, head, feet, and wing area.

*The Harpy eagle's eyesight is so sharp that even in flight, the bird can spot prey in the jungle canopy. The eye ridges or "brows" that make an eagle look so fierce help shade the bird's eyes from glaring sunlight.*

⑥ Fill in the eyes and beak as shown. Add feathered texture around the bird, using longer strokes for the wings and shorter, fainter strokes around the head, body, and upper legs. Give the bird's feet ridges with short, horizontal lines and add dimension to the claws by shading as shown.

*The Harpy eagle has especially thick toes and large claws capable of clutching prey as heavy as deer.*

**DRAWING TIP:** One purpose of a bird's feathers is to smooth the shape of the bird so that it slips through the air easily in flight. Notice how each feather overlaps others around it, making a sleek, fanlike pattern.

# The Common Marmoset of South America is one of the smallest monkeys in the world.

① Begin by drawing a rounded, rectangular body.

*There are many different species of marmoset. The common marmoset's body is about 10 inches in length.*

② Then draw an oval for the head and mane, and sketch a smaller circle for the upper hindleg. From the base of the body extend a long line with a slight curve at the end for the marmoset's tail.

*The marmoset lives in the very tops of tall jungle trees. This primate seldom, if ever, touches the ground.*

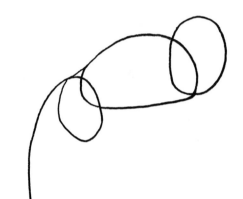

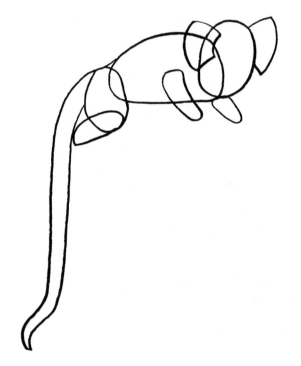

③ On either side of the head draw two fan-shaped ears. Add two small arms and a lower leg. Then draw a line for the underside of the tail, narrowing it until it reaches the tip.

*The tail of the common marmoset is longer than its body. Unlike the tails of some other monkeys, the common marmoset's tail is not prehensile, or grasping.*

**MORE SCIENCE:** Marmosets come in a variety of colors with different-shaped fur collars and crests. The common marmoset is easy to recognize because of its striped black-and-white fur and its white ear tufts.

**The name marmoset comes from a French word meaning "small boy" or "dwarf."**

④ Now draw the small, oblong eye mask and the teardrop-shaped muzzle. Add the far hindleg (which will rest on a branch) as well as the small shapes for the feet.

*Because of their gentle ways and small size, thousands of marmosets and their relatives, the tamarins, have been captured and used for pets.*

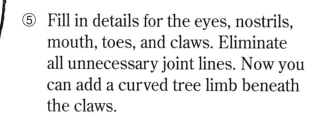

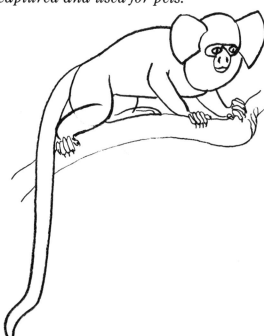

⑤ Fill in details for the eyes, nostrils, mouth, toes, and claws. Eliminate all unnecessary joint lines. Now you can add a curved tree limb beneath the claws.

*The marmoset has long, curved claws on all but its innermost toe, unlike most monkeys, which have flattened nails.*

⑥ Soften all of the edges around the marmoset by using short, light lines to indicate fur. Use darker strokes around the face and along the back and tail to show striped fur. Shade in fur patches on the underside of the body and detail the ear, feet, and hands with very light markings.

*As a tree dweller, a marmoset must know how to grasp firmly. From birth, a baby marmoset can hold tightly to its mother's fur. It then learns how to grasp tree branches. It uses its claws to grip bark much the same way a squirrel does.*

# The Marine Iguana lives on a few small islands off the west coast of Ecuador in South America. It is

① To begin your marine iguana, draw a long oval for the body.

*The marine iguana is about three to four feet long, not including its muscular tail.*

② Draw a long, rounded shape for the head and neck, small ovals for the upper legs, and a curved tail line.

*Despite its fierce appearance, the marine iguana lives entirely on seaweed. When threatened, however, the lizard assumes an attack posture, standing high on its legs and puffing out its throat.*

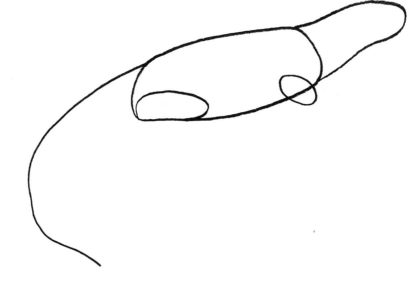

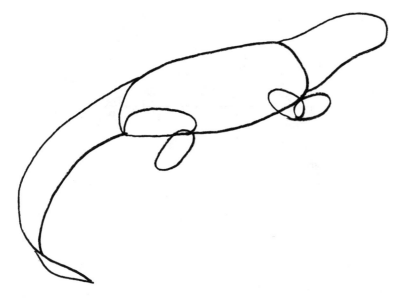

③ Now sketch in two lower legs and a curved line for the underside of the tail. Be sure to add the small tip of the tail that curls around.

*When it swims, the marine iguana keeps its feet tucked in and moves forward by swishing its body and tail from side to side.*

**MORE SCIENCE:** While other iguanas and their eggs are still hunted for food on the mainland of Central America and South America, the marine iguanas on the Galápagos Islands are now a protected species.

**the only true marine lizard, one that regularly swims and depends on the sea for its food.**

---

④ Sketch guidelines for the sharp tips that run along the neck, back, and tail of the iguana. Add a curved line to indicate the head and two rounded shapes for the large feet.

*Usually iguanas gather peacefully in large groups to sun themselves on rocks. However, at breeding time, the males fight over females by butting each other with their bumpy heads.*

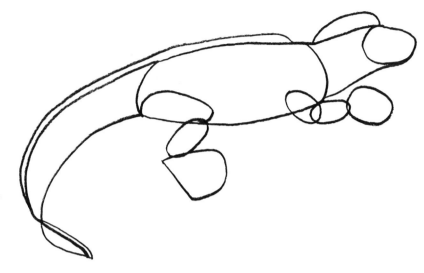

⑤ Add the toes and claws, the small head spikes, the eye, the small nostril, the ear hole, and the mouth. Eliminate all unnecessary lines to create a smooth outline. Begin to add texture along the underside of the neck and body.

*The fringe along the iguana's back is made of tough flesh.*

⑥ Sketch in the marine iguana's jagged fringe along its head, body, and tail. Erase the guidelines. Draw light hatch marks and dark, short strokes to create a wrinkled, splotchy pattern on the lizard's neck and body. Add ridges with small, dark spots along the tail. Finally, complete your creature by adding textured markings around its face.

*The texture of the marine iguana's skin is similar to that of other lizards. The background coloring is normally dark, and skin patches can be dark red, gray, or brown.*

# The Quetzal is one of the most colorful birds on Earth. Its iridescent-green tail plumes, which can be more than three feet

① Draw an egg-shaped body at an angle as shown.

*Quetzals feed mainly on fruits. They live in the wooded mountains that extend from southern Mexico to Panama.*

② Continue drawing your quetzal by adding a head on top and a loop at the bottom of the body.

*The quetzal has a strong beak, which it uses to carve out decaying tree trunks to make its nest.*

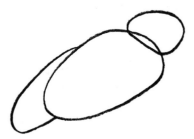

③ Now draw a long, curved tail that flairs out toward the bottom. Add the two small feet.

*The quetzal is the symbol of Guatemala, and the Guatemalan dollar is called a quetzal.*

**MORE SCIENCE:** The quetzal is the most famous of a group of birds called trogons, who are known for their brightly colored feathers.

**long, were once collected by ancient Mayan and Aztec peoples of Mexico. The plumes were woven into elaborate ritual headdresses.**

④ Sketch in the feathers, an eye, and a small triangular beak. If you want to, add a branch under the bird's feet. Now eliminate all unnecessary lines.

*Although laws protect the endangered quetzal, poachers still hunt them for their beautiful feathers.*

⑤ Add fine lines close together for the feathers around the head and body. Erase any hard lines that aren't needed. Last, darken the areas near the eye and beak, and fill in the eye and the ends of the feathers.

*Young quetzals remain in the nest until they learn to become strong fliers.*

# The Kangaroo is the national symbol of Australia. Perhaps best known for its spectacular jumping ability, the

① Begin your jumping kangaroo by drawing a pear-shaped body that's flattened along the bottom for the animal's underside.

*The gray kangaroo, the one you are drawing here, is well known around the world. Gray kangaroos may grow to six feet tall when standing fully erect. The head and body length can be as long as five feet. Their smallest cousins are the rat kangaroos, which are only 16 inches long.*

② Curve the tail upward from the body. Draw an elongated oval for the head and another smaller one for the upper foreleg.

*The kangaroo uses its muscular tail for balance as it hops along (the tail keeps the kangaroo from falling forward). This marsupial also will lower its tail to the ground and lean back on it to rest.*

③ Sketch the hindlegs and lower forelegs.

*The kangaroo uses its hindlegs to hop at speeds of up to 40 miles per hour.*

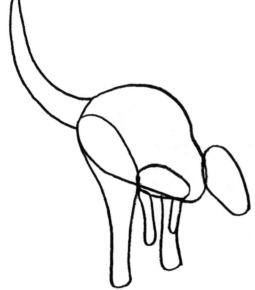

**MORE SCIENCE:** Kangaroos, unlike most mammals, keep growing all their lives. The older they are, the bigger they are!

**kangaroo is the largest marsupial—pouched mammal—in the world.**

④ Now draw two banana-shaped hindfeet and connect them to the hindlegs. Add ears and two small shapes to define the front claws.

*The kangaroo's large ears turn in all directions to hear predators, such as wild dogs or eagles, that prey on kangaroos.*

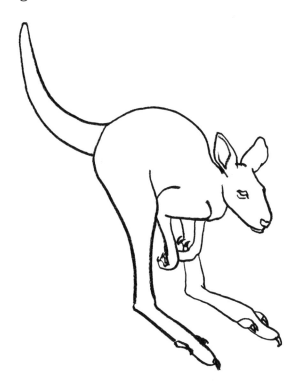

⑤ Draw the eye, nose, mouth, toes and claws, and the inside of the ear. Erase the unnecessary lines around the feet, body, head, and legs.

*A kangaroo's hindfoot has one long middle toe, another toe on the outside of each foot, and two toes together on the inside of each foot. The kangaroo uses its middle toe as a weapon in fights, and it grooms itself with its long claws.*

⑥ Shade in the kangaroo's body, head, and legs to create a furry texture. Make the fur lines longer on the body and shorter and smoother on the legs and tail. Don't forget to fill in the eye and add whiskers on the snout.

*A kangaroo's fur is thick and can be fairly long. Depending on the species, fur color may be reddish brown or dark brown with paler fur on the chest and stomach. Your gray kangaroo, of course, has gray fur!*

# The Great White Shark is feared around the world as the most dangerous of all sea creatures. The largest of the

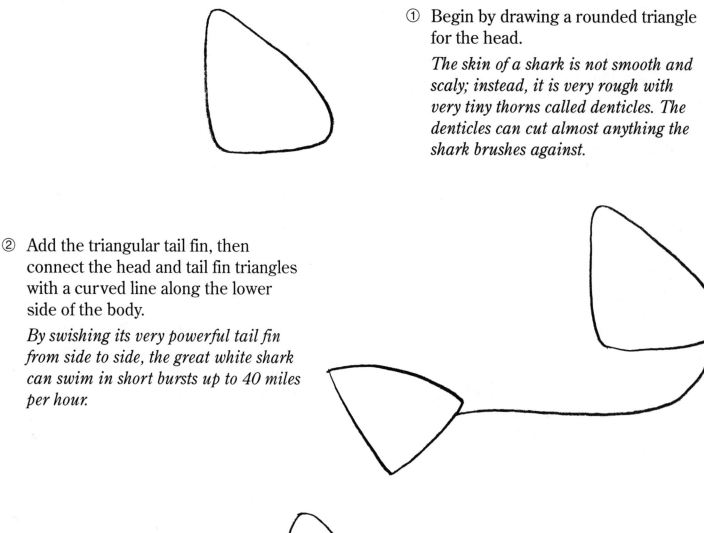

① Begin by drawing a rounded triangle for the head.

*The skin of a shark is not smooth and scaly; instead, it is very rough with very tiny thorns called denticles. The denticles can cut almost anything the shark brushes against.*

② Add the triangular tail fin, then connect the head and tail fin triangles with a curved line along the lower side of the body.

*By swishing its very powerful tail fin from side to side, the great white shark can swim in short bursts up to 40 miles per hour.*

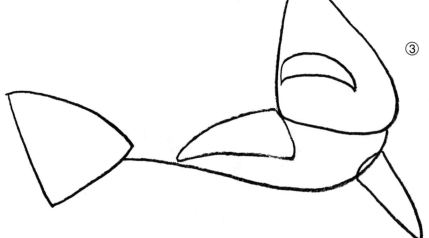

③ Next sketch in the crescent-moon shaped mouth and the two large pectoral fins.

*Unlike the soft, flowing fins of other fish, the fins of the great white are tough and extremely sharp along the edges.*

**MORE SCIENCE:** Sharks do occasionally kill people, but worldwide there are only about six deaths of this kind each year.

**carnivorous fish, the great white, like all sharks, is one of the oldest kinds of animals still living on Earth. Scientists think the first sharks lived 400 million years ago.**

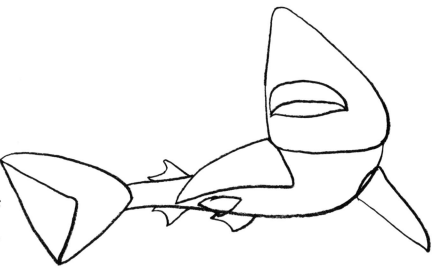

④ Now draw a line for the top edge of the body. Add two small fins toward the shark's tail and two other fins underneath the animal. Add a notch in the tail fin and a curving line for the lower edge of the mouth.

*The great white is a meat eater. When it opens its jaws to bite, a covering slips over its eyes to protect them while the animal attacks. The jaws slide forward so they can open as wide as possible.*

⑤ Draw all five gill slits, a nostril, an eye, a crease above the upper jaw, and several rows of sharp, triangular teeth. Erase the unnecessary lines around the jaw, fins, and tail.

*To breathe, the great white shark takes water into its mouth, then forces it past the gills and out the gill slits. As the water passes the gills, oxygen from the water is absorbed into the shark's bloodstream.*

⑥ Using short, dark strokes, shade the body smoothly. The great white, like most sharks, is darker on the top and white on the underside. Last, darken the eye and the gaping mouth.

*The great white shark has narrow teeth on its bottom jaw for grabbing prey and wider, saw-edged teeth on its top jaw for cutting through huge pieces of flesh. As with all sharks, the great white doesn't chew its food, but simply bites and swallows.*

# Bringing Your Animal to Life

Here are more tips on how to put life into your drawings. Keep in mind that the most realistic drawings combine several finishing techniques. You can practice and experiment with your own favorite combinations!

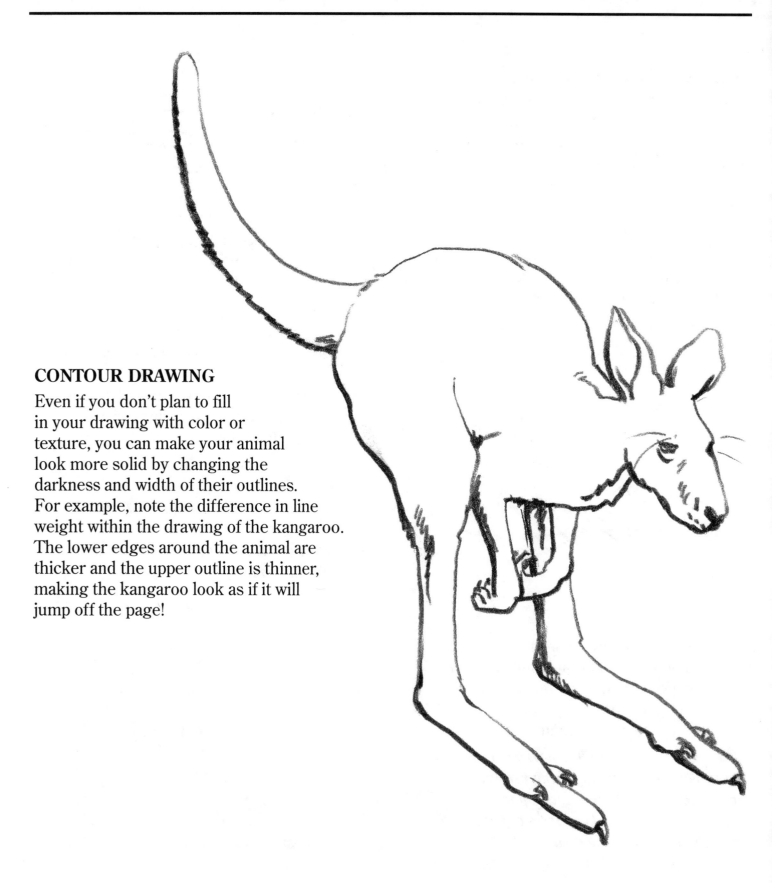

## CONTOUR DRAWING

Even if you don't plan to fill in your drawing with color or texture, you can make your animal look more solid by changing the darkness and width of their outlines. For example, note the difference in line weight within the drawing of the kangaroo. The lower edges around the animal are thicker and the upper outline is thinner, making the kangaroo look as if it will jump off the page!

## CAST SHADOWS

Your drawings will look much more realistic if some ground is added for the animals to stand on. Begin drawing a horizontal line at ground level. Then thicken the line to make it look like a full shadow, as shown in the drawing of the hippopotamus. Make the shadow thinner under narrow body parts (like the hippo's small tail!) and thicker under fuller body parts. Shadows can also appear on the underside of the animal itself, not just on the ground. With a fish or a flying bird, you can show the shadow falling on the ground or ocean floor—even if it doesn't touch the animal itself.

## LIGHT FIGURE, DARK BACKGROUND

You'll be surprised by how rounded your animal looks if you simply darken the space behind it. You can imagine the animal standing at the edge of a dark forest or swimming in front of an underwater cavern. Of course, if you add some shadows underneath the animal, the effect is even stronger—as with this raccoon!

# Making Your Animal Seem Larger (or Smaller)

How do you make an animal in a small drawing seem larger? Or an animal in a huge picture seem smaller?

## THE HORIZON LINE

To show how big your creature is in a drawing, add a ground or horizon line across your picture. The horizon line is on the viewer's eye level. So, if the horizon is near the bottom of your page and the animal stretches far above it, like with this elephant, the viewer will imagine it as large. If you draw in a horizon line near the top section of your picture, your elephant will appear much smaller.

## ADDING OBJECTS

Another way is to include objects whose size most people know. Fully grown trees, for instance, are usually much larger than humans. Thus, if you include a large tree trunk near an average-sized deer, the viewer will assume the animal is about the size of a person. Conversely, if you draw a big flower towering over an elephant, the viewer will see your elephant as tiny!

## POINT OF VIEW

You can also show the approximate size of an animal by drawing it from a person's perspective. For instance, if you were standing next to a skunk, you would look down on its back and the top of its head. You will need to find a photo or a model of the animal with the point of view you want and draw it that way. It's trickier than most of the other hints in this book, but you'll love the effect!

# Tips on Color

**Your picture will stand out from the rest of the crowd if you use these helpful tips on how to add color to your masterpiece!**

---

## TRY WHITE ON BLACK

For a different look, try working on black construction paper or art paper. Then instead of a pencil, use white chalk, white prismacolor pencil, or poster paint. With this technique, you'll need to concentrate on drawing the light areas in your picture rather than shadows.

## TRY BLACK AND WHITE ON GRAY (OR TAN)

You don't need special gray or tan paper from the art store. Try cutting apart the inside of a grocery bag or a cereal box instead. This time, your background is a middle tone. Sketch your animal in black, then use white to make highlights. Add black for the shadows. Don't completely cover up the tan or gray of the cardboard. Let it be the middle tone. With this technique, your pictures can have a very finished look with a minimal amount of drawing!

## TRY COLOR

Instead of using every color in your marker set or your colored pencil set, try drawing in black for shadows, white for highlights, and one color for a middle tone. This third color blended with the white creates a fourth color. You will be surprised how professional your drawing will look.

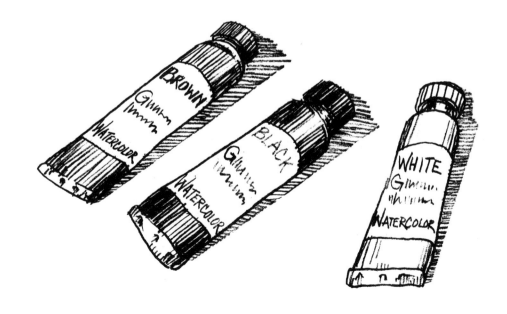

63